5 Ingredient Cookbook

Hannie P. Scott

CONTENTS

ACKNOWLEDGMENTS

I am so grateful for those of you who make up the community of readers that I love to write recipe books for! Thank you for your shares, encouraging emails, feedback, and reviews. I appreciate each one more than you guys know!

**A special thanks to...
-Jan
-Cheryl
-Ann Marie
-Cindy
-Jennie
-Charlie
-Vicki

This book wouldn't be possible without you!

Chicken and Waffle Sliders

Servings: 6

What you need:
12 frozen mini waffles, toasted
6 chicken tenders, cooked
Maple syrup
Toothpicks

What to do:
1. Slice the cooked chicken tenders into thirds.
2. Sandwich chicken pieces between two mini waffles and secure with a toothpick.
3. Serve with maple syrup.

Buffalo Chicken Dip

Servings: 8-10

What you need:
3 chicken breasts, cooked and shredded
8 oz cream cheese, softened
1 cup ranch dressing
1 cup Frank's hot sauce
1 cup shredded cheddar cheese

What to do:
1. Mix together the cream cheese, ranch dressing, hot sauce, and cheddar cheese in a slow cooker.
2. Place shredded chicken into the mixture and combine.
3. Place the lid on the slow cooker and heat on high for 1-2 hours.
4. Serve straight from your slow cooker on warm setting or pour it into a serving dish when ready to serve.
5. This can be served with veggie slices, chips, crackers, etc.

Chicken Salad

Servings: 2

What you need:
1 cup cooked and shredded chicken breast
2 tbsp pickle relish
1/3 cup mayonnaise
1/4 tsp paprika
Salt and pepper, to taste

What to do:
1.   In a large bowl, combine all ingredients.
2.   Mix very well, until everything is combined.
3.   Cover and refrigerate for at least 2 hours.

Chicken Fingers

Servings: 4

What you need:
4 chicken breasts, cut into strips
1 egg, beaten
1 cup all-purpose flour
2 tsp Cajun seasoning

What to do:
1. Preheat your oven to 425 degrees F and line a baking sheet with parchment paper.
2. In a shallow dish, combine the flour with the Cajun seasoning.
3. Place the beaten egg in a separate shallow dish.
4. Dip each chicken strip into the egg then the flour mixture until well coated.
5. Place strips on the baking sheet and bake for 18-20 minutes. Turn once halfway through cooking.

Buffalo Chicken Sliders

Servings: 10

What you need:
3 chicken breasts
1 12-oz bottle of buffalo wing sauce, divided
1 package of ranch seasoning mix
2 packs of Hawaiian rolls
1 package coleslaw mix

What to do:
1. Place the chicken breasts into your slow cooker and pour in ¾ of the wing sauce and all of the ranch seasoning mix. Cover and cook for 6-7 hours or until the chicken easily shreds.
2. Once the chicken is cooked, drain off the liquid.
3. Add rest of the buffalo sauce and shred the chicken with two forks.
4. Spoon the shredded chicken onto Hawaiian rolls, top with coleslaw mix, and serve.

Honey Chicken

Servings: 4-6

What you need:
4 chicken breasts
1/3 cup melted butter
1/3 cup honey
2 tbsp spicy brown mustard
1/4 tsp salt

What to do:
1. Preheat your oven to 350 degrees F.
2. Place the chicken breasts in a shallow square baking pan.
3. Combine the butter, honey, mustard, and salt in a small bowl. Pour this mixture over the chicken.
4. Bake for 1 hour or to a minimal internal temperature of 165 degrees F. Baste every 15 minutes while baking.

Maple Mustard Baked Chicken

Servings: 4

What you need:
4 chicken breasts
1/2 cup spicy brown mustard
1/4 cup maple syrup
1 tbsp red wine vinegar
Salt and pepper, to taste

What to do:
1. Preheat your oven to 425 degrees F.
2. In a medium sized bowl, mix together the mustard, syrup, and vinegar.
3. Place the chicken into a 9x13 baking dish and season with salt and pepper.
4. Pour the mustard mixture over the chicken.
5. Bake for 30-40 minutes or until the internal temperature of the chicken reaches 165 degrees F.

Easy Italian Baked Chicken

Servings: 4

What you need:
4 chicken breasts
1 packet dry Italian dressing mix
1/2 cup packed brown sugar

What to do:
1. Preheat your oven to 350 degrees and line a 9x13 baking dish with aluminum foil.
2. In a small bowl, mix together the Italian dressing mix and the brown sugar.
3. Place the chicken breasts between two sheets of wax or parchment paper and pound them until they are thin.
4. Cut each chicken breast in half.
5. Dip each piece of chicken into the Italian dressing/sugar mixture and coat well.
6. Place the chicken into the baking pan.
7. Sprinkle any remaining seasoning mixture onto the chicken.
8. Bake for 20-30 minutes or until the internal temp is 165 degrees F. Flip the chicken over after about 15 minutes.
9. Broil the chicken on each side for 1-2 minutes before removing from the oven.

Chicken and Cheese Rolls

Servings: 6

What you need:
1 package 6-count refrigerated crescent rolls
2 cups chopped cooked chicken
2 cups shredded cheddar cheese
1 10.75-oz can of cream of chicken soup
1 cup of milk

What to do:
1. Preheat your oven to 350 degrees F and spray a baking dish with non-stick spray.
2. Separate the crescent rolls and unroll them onto a clean surface.
3. In a medium bowl, mix together the cream of chicken soup and milk.
4. Place a spoonful of chicken and a spoonful of cheese on the large part of each crescent roll.
5. Roll each crescent roll up and pinch the seal together.
6. Place each roll in the prepared baking dish.
7. Pour the soup mixture over the rolls.
8. Bake for 30 minutes.

Barbeque Chicken Legs

Servings: 4-6

What you need:
3 lbs chicken legs
2 cups of your favorite barbeque sauce
Garlic powder
Cajun Seasoning
Salt and pepper

What to do:
1.   Preheat your oven to 350 degrees F.
2.   Pat the chicken dry with a paper towel and season well with garlic powder, Cajun seasoning, salt and pepper.
3.   Place the chicken on a rack inside of a roasting pan.
4.   Cover the roasting pan and bake for 45 minutes.
5.   Remove the chicken from the oven and brush each piece generously with barbeque sauce.
6.   Bake uncovered for 30 more minutes.
7.   Increase the heat to 450 degrees and cook for another 5 minutes.

Slow Cooker Mexican Chicken

Servings: 4

What you need:
4 chicken breasts
1 tbsp taco seasoning
1/2 cup enchilada sauce
1 cup shredded cheddar cheese
3 green onions, chopped

What to do:
1. Add the chicken, taco seasoning, and enchilada sauce to your slow cooker and cook on low for 4-6 hours.
2. Shred chicken with a fork.
3. Stir in cheese and cook for another hour.
4. Stir in green onions before serving.

Chicken Cordon Bleu

Servings: 6

What you need:
6 thin sliced chicken breasts
1/3 lb thinly sliced black forest ham
1/3 lb thinly sliced Swiss cheese
Salt and pepper, to taste

What to do:
1. Preheat your oven to 350 degrees F.
2. Lay the chicken breasts out on a large cutting board or other clean working surface.
3. Season each breast with salt and pepper.
4. Lay 1-2 slices of ham on each breast.
5. Lay 2 slices of cheese on top of the ham.
6. Roll up each chicken breast tightly and secure with toothpicks.
7. Place each rolled up chicken breast onto a baking pan and bake for 30-35 minutes.

Shredded Buffalo Chicken

Servings: 4

What you need:
4 chicken breasts
12 oz bottle of buffalo wing sauce
2 tbsp ranch mix
2 tbsp butter
2 cloves garlic, minced

What to do:
1.   Place the chicken breasts in your slow cooker.
2.   Pour the wing sauce over the chicken.
3.   Sprinkle ranch mix over the sauce.
4.   Add butter and garlic to the slow cooker.
5.   Cook on low for 4-6 hours or until chicken shreds easily.
6.   Remove chicken from the slow cooker and shred it completely.
7.   Put the shredded chicken back into the slow cooker and cook on low for another hour before serving.

Slow Cooker Chicken Salsa Verde

Servings: 6

What you need:
6 chicken breasts
2 cups salsa verde
1 bottle of beer or 12 oz of chicken broth
2 tsp cumin
1 small can green chiles

What to do:
1. Place the chicken in your slow cooker and pour on the salsa verde and the beer or broth.
2. Sprinkle the chicken with cumin and pour the chiles on top.
3. Cook for 8 hours on low or 4 hours on high.
4. Shred the chicken with a fork.

Slow Cooker Shredded BBQ Chicken

Servings: 4

What you need:
3 chicken breasts, cut in half
1 12-oz bottle of barbeque sauce
1/2 cup Italian dressing
1/4 cup brown sugar
2 tbsp Worcestershire sauce

What to do:
1.   Place the chicken in your slow cooker.
2.   In a medium bowl, whisk together the barbeque sauce, Italian dressing, brown sugar, and Worcestershire sauce.
3.   Pour this mixture over the chicken.
4.   Cook for 6-8 hours on low or 4 hours on high.
5.   Shred the chicken with two forks.

Slow Cooker Mexican Chicken

Servings: 4

What you need:
4 chicken breasts
1 tbsp taco seasoning
1/2 cup enchilada sauce
1 cup shredded cheddar cheese
3 green onions, chopped

What to do:
1. Add the chicken, taco seasoning, and enchilada sauce to a slow cooker and cook on low for 4-6 hours.
2. Shred chicken with a fork.
3. Stir in cheese and cook for another hour.
4. Stir in green onions before serving.

Slow Cooker Buffalo Ranch Wings

Servings: 4

What you need:
12-14 chicken wings
1 12-oz bottle of Frank's Red Hot Sauce
1 packet ranch dry seasoning

What to do:
1. Place the chicken wings in your slow cooker.
2. Cover and cook on high for 2-3 hours.
3. After 2-3 hours, drain the liquid out of the slow cooker.
4. In a small bowl, mix together the ranch seasoning and the hot sauce.
5. Pour this mixture over the chicken in the slow cooker.
6. Cover and cook for 1 hour.
7. Serve with your choice of dipping sauce.

Slow Cooker Teriyaki Chicken

Servings: 2

What you need:
2 boneless, skinless chicken breasts
1 1/2 cups teriyaki Sauce
2 cups cooked rice

What to do:
1.   Pound out the chicken until it is uniformly thin.
2.   Lay the chicken breasts in the bottom of your slow cooker and cover with teriyaki sauce.
3.   Cook on low for 6 hours or until chicken is tender and cooked.
4.   Serve with rice.

Slow Cooker BBQ Ribs

Servings: 4

What you need:
2 1/2 lb rack of baby back pork ribs
1 tbsp brown sugar
Salt and pepper
1 1/2 cups BBQ sauce

What to do:
1. Season the ribs with salt, pepper, and brown sugar.
2. Place the rack of ribs in your slow cooker with the more meaty side facing the wall of the slow cooker. You will have to bend it and wrap it around the inside.
3. Pour BBQ sauce over the ribs.
4. Cook on low for 8 hours.

Slow Cooker 5-ingredient Chili

Servings: 6

What you need:
1 lb ground beef, browned and drained
3 15-oz cans rotel tomatoes
2 15-oz cans beans, drained (kidney or chili or both)
1 small white onion, diced
2 tbsp chili powder

What to do:
1.   Add all of the ingredients to your slow cooker.
2.   Cook on low for 6 hours.

Slow Cooker Orange Chicken

Servings: 4

What you need:
3/4 cup orange marmalade
1 cup honey BBQ sauce
2 tbsp soy sauce
3 boneless, skinless chicken breasts
Cooked rice

What to do:
1. Cut the chicken into bite sized pieces.
2. Place chicken pieces, marmalade, BBQ sauce, and soy sauce in a slow cooker and cook on low for 4 hours.
3. Serve over rice.

Slow Cooker Hawaiian BBQ Chicken

Servings: 6

What you need:
6 boneless, skinless chicken breasts
1 bottle Hawaiian style BBQ sauce
1 20 oz. can pineapple chunks

What to do:
1. Spray the inside of your slow cooker with cooking spray or insert a liner.
2. Place the chicken breasts in the slow cooker and cover with the BBQ sauce.
3. Pour the pineapple chunks on top of the chicken.
4. Cook on high for 2-3 hours or on low for 4-6 hours.
5. Shred the chicken with 2 forks then serve.

Slow Cooker Apricot Orange Chicken

Servings: 4

What you need:
4 boneless, skinless chicken breasts
1 18-oz jar apricot preserves
1 cup orange juice
1 package onion soup mix

What to do:
1.   Place the chicken in your slow cooker.
2.   Stir together the preserves, orange juice, and onion soup mix in a small bowl.
3.   Pour the mixture over the chicken.
4.   Cook on low for 6 hours or until the chicken is very tender.

Slow Cooker Honey Garlic Chicken

Servings: 4

What you need:
4 boneless, skinless chicken breasts
1/2 cup A1 steak sauce
1/4 cup honey
1 tsp garlic powder
1/2 tsp hot sauce

What to do:
1.   Place the chicken in your slow cooker.
2.   Mix the steak sauce, honey, garlic powder, and hot sauce together in a small bowl.
3.   Pour the mixture over the chicken.
4.   Cook on low for 6 hours or until chicken is done and tender.

Slow Cooker Tangy Meatballs

Servings: 6

What you need:
28 oz of frozen fully cooked meatballs
18 oz jar of grape jelly
12 oz jar of chili sauce
1 tsp ground mustard

What to do:
1.	Place all of the ingredients to your slow cooker.
2.	Cook on low for 4 hours, stirring occasionally.

Slow Cooker Italian Chicken

Servings: 4

What you need:
4 boneless, skinless chicken breasts
1 can cheddar cheese soup
8 oz of zesty Italian dressing

What to do:
1. Add all 3 of the ingredients to your slow cooker.
2. Cook for 6 hours on low, stirring every couple of hours.

Slow Cooker Ranch Roast Beef

Servings: 6

What you need:
3lb boneless chuck roast
1 packet ranch seasoning
1 tsp garlic salt
6 French rolls
6 slices mozzarella cheese

What to do:
1. Place the chuck roast, ranch seasoning, and garlic salt in your slow cooker and cook for 8 hours on low.
2. Shred the beef with 2 forks and serve on French rolls topped with mozzarella cheese.

Slow Cooker Mexican Chicken II

Servings: 4

What you need:
4 boneless, skinless chicken breasts
1 16-oz jar of salsa
1 15-oz can black beans, drained and rinsed
1 package taco seasoning

What to do:
1. Place all of the ingredients except the black beans into your slow cooker.
2. Cook on low for 8 hours. Stir every 2 hours.
3. One hour before serving, pour in the black beans.

Slow Cooker Spicy Meatballs

Servings: 6

What you need:
1 28-oz bag of fully cooked frozen meatballs
12 oz grape jelly
28 oz bbq sauce
2 habanero peppers

What to do:
1.   Dice the habanero peppers very finely. Wear gloves!
2.   Place all of the ingredients into your slow cooker.
3.   Cook for 4 hours on low.

Slow Cooker Chicken and Cheese

Servings: 4

What you need:
4 boneless, skinless chicken breasts
1 16-oz jar of salsa
4 slices provolone cheese

What to do:
1. Place the chicken breasts and salsa in your slow cooker. Cook for 4-5 hours or until the center of the chicken is no longer pink.
2. Spoon salsa over the top of the chicken and place a slice of cheese on each piece.

Slow Cooker Ham

Servings: 4

What you need:
1 precooked, spiral cut ham
2 cups brown sugar
1 can pineapple rings

What to do:
1. Sprinkle 1 and 1/2 cups of the brown sugar into the bottom of a slow cooker.
2. Place the ham on top of the brown sugar and pour the pineapple rings and juice on top.
3. Sprinkle the rest of the brown sugar on top of the ham.
4. Cook for 6-8 hours on low.

Slow Cooker Pulled Pork

Servings: 4

What you need:
2-lb pork tenderloin
1 can root beer
1 18-oz bottle of bbq sauce

What to do:
1. Place the tenderloin in the slow cooker and pour the can of root beer over it.
2. Cook on low for 6 hours or until the pork shreds easily.
3. Drain off most of the root beer and shred pork completely with a fork.
4. Pour the bbq sauce over the pork and stir.
5. Cook on low for another hour or two before serving.

Slow Cooker Beef Burritos

Servings: 4

What you need:
2 lbs stew meat
1 large can enchilada sauce
1 beef bouillon
7 tortillas, burrito size
1 cup shredded cheddar cheese

What to do:
1. Place beef, enchilada sauce, and beef bouillon in the slow cooker and cook on low for 7-8 hours.
2. Shred the beef with a fork.
3. Spoon beef mixture onto each tortilla, add a couple tbsp of cheese to each, and roll up.
4. Place each burrito in a baking dish and broil for 3-4 minutes.

Slow Cooker Garlic Tilapia

Servings: 4

What you need:
4 tilapia filets
2 tbsp butter
1 tbsp minced garlic
Salt and pepper, to taste

What to do:
1.   Place the tilapia filets on a large sheet of aluminum foil.
2.   Generously season each filet with salt and pepper.
3.   Divide the butter and garlic between the four filets and top each of them.
4.   Wrap the foil around the fish, sealing it as tightly as possible.
5.   Place in your slow cooker and cook on high for 2 hours.

Slow Cooker Pork Chops

Servings: 6

What you need:
6 pork chops
1 package ranch dressing mix
2 cans cream of mushroom soup

What to do:
1.   Place all of the ingredients into your slow cooker.
2.   Cook on low for 7-8 hours, stirring occasionally.

Slow Cooker Sweet Potatoes

Servings: 4

What you need:
4 medium sized sweet potatoes
Butter
Brown sugar
Mini marshmallows

What to do:
1.   Scrub, wash, and dry the sweet potatoes.
2.   Poke each potato with a fork several times.
3.   Wrap each potato in foil twice.
4.   Place potatoes in slow cooker and cook on high for 4 hours or on low for 8 hours.
5.   Top with butter, brown sugar, and mini marshmallows before serving.

Slow Cooker Spinach Queso Dip

Servings: 6-8

What you need:
10 oz frozen chopped spinach, thawed and drained well
1 lb Velveeta cheese
8 oz cream cheese
1 jar salsa

What to do:
1. Cut the Velveeta and cream cheese into cubes and place them into a slow cooker.
2. Add in the spinach and salsa.
3. Cook for 3-4 hours on low, stirring every hour or so.
4. Serve with tortilla chips.

Slow Cooker Cheddar Creamed Corn

Servings: 6

What you need:
32-oz of frozen corn
1 8-oz block of cream cheese, cubed
1 cup shredded cheddar cheese
1/4 cup butter
1/2 cup heavy cream

What to do:
1.   Place all of the ingredients in your slow cooker and stir well.
2.   Cook on low for 3-4 hours or until cream cheese is melted.
3.   Stir well and serve.

Roasted Cauliflower

Servings: 4

What you need:
1 large head of cauliflower
3 tbsp olive oil
1 clove garlic, minced
1 tsp sea salt
2 tbsp grated parmesan cheese

What to do:
1. Preheat your oven to 350 degrees F.
2. Spray a baking dish with non-stick cooking spray.
3. Trim the stem of the cauliflower so that it is even with the cauliflower florets and the cauliflower sits flat.
4. In a small bowl, stir together the olive oil and the garlic.
5. Brush the bottom of the cauliflower with the olive oil/garlic mixture then season with salt.
6. Lay the cauliflower flat in the baking dish and brush the top and sides with the olive oil mixture and season with salt and parmesan cheese.
7. Bake for 55 minutes to 1 hour or until the center of the cauliflower is tender when pierced with a knife.
8. Slice into wedges before serving.

Kale Chips

Servings: 4

What you need:
1 bunch kale, washed and thoroughly dried
1 tbsp olive oil
2 tsp sea salt
1/2 of a lemon

What to do:
1. Preheat your oven to 300 degrees F.
2. Strip the kale from the stems and break into it pieces.
3. In a large bowl, combine the kale with olive oil and salt.
4. Spread kale evenly on large baking sheet.
5. Bake for 20 minutes or until kale is crispy.
6. Remove from oven and squeeze lemon juice over the kale chips (watch for seeds!)
7. Serve immediately.

Veggie Wrap

Servings: 1

What you need:
1 low carb wrap
3 tbsp cream cheese
2 cups chopped veggies
1 tbsp lemon juice

What to do:
1. Spread cream cheese on the wrap.
2. Chop all the veggies into small pieces and place them In a large bowl.
3. Spritz veggies with lemon juice to preserve colors (and for flavor!).
4. Place the veggies on wrap and roll it up.
5. Cut the wrap in half or in thirds.

Slow Cooker Cocktail Sausages

Servings: 6

What you need:
2 14-oz packages of cocktail smokies
18 oz jar of grape jelly
12 oz jar of chili sauce
1 tsp ground mustard

What to do:
1. Place all of the ingredients to your slow cooker.
2. Cook on low for 4 hours, stirring occasionally.

Slow Cooker Corn on the Cob

Servings: 6

What you need:
6 ears of corn
1/2 stick of butter
Salt and pepper, to taste

What to do:
1. Lightly spread butter on each corn cob.
2. Sprinkle each cob with salt and pepper.
3. Wrap each corn cob in aluminum foil.
4. Place them all in the slow cooker and cook for 2 hours.

Zucchini Chips

Servings: 2

What you need:
1 large zucchini
1 tsp olive oil
Salt to taste

What to do:
1.   Very thinly slice the zucchini.
2.   Place slices on baking sheet.
3.   Brush on the olive oil.
4.   Bake at 225 degrees F for 2 hours.

Mashed Cauliflower

Servings: 2

What you need:
1 head of cauliflower
1 clove garlic, minced
2 tbsp butter
Salt and pepper, to taste

What to do:
1.	Cut the cauliflower into medium sized florets.
2.	Place the florets into a soup pot and cover them with water.
3.	Bring the water to a boil and keep it at a medium boil for 15-20 minutes.
4.	Drain the water from the pot and turn the heat to low.
5.	Mast the cauliflower in the pot with a potato masher.
6.	Add the garlic, butter, salt, and pepper and stir well.

Sausage, Egg, and Cheese Roll-Ups

Servings: 6-8

What you need:
5 eggs
1 can crescent rolls
8 fully cooked sausage links
4 slices cheese
Salt and pepper, to taste

What to do:
1. Heat your oven to 350 degrees F.
2. Line a baking pan with parchment paper.
3. Beat the eggs in a small bowl and scramble all but 2 tbsp of them.
4. Unroll the crescent rolls onto the parchment paper.
5. Cut the cheese slices in half and place a half on each roll.
6. Top each slice of cheese with a spoonful of scrambled eggs and 1 sausage link.
7. Loosely roll up the crescent rolls.
8. Brush each roll with the reserved eggs and sprinkle with salt and pepper.
9. Bake for 15-18 minutes or until the rolls are golden-brown.

Waffle Biscuits

Servings: 4

What you need:
1 8-count can of flaky biscuits
4 eggs, fried or scrambled
4 slices of cheese
8 slices of bacon, cooked

What to do:
1. Heat and spray your waffle maker with non-stick spray.
2. Unroll the biscuits from the can.
3. Place one biscuit in the center of your waffle maker, close the lid and cook for 2-3 minutes or until the biscuit Is golden brown. Repeat until all 8 biscuits are cooked.
4. Place 1 egg, 1 slice of cheese, and 2 slices of bacon on a waffle biscuit and top with another waffle biscuit. Repeat until you have assembled 4 waffle biscuits.
5. Serve warm.

Slow Cooker Broccoli Casserole

Servings: 6

What you need:
2 12-oz bags of frozen broccoli florets
2 cans cheddar cheese soup
1 cup shredded cheddar cheese
Salt and pepper, to taste

What to do:
1.   Slightly thaw the broccoli.
2.   Combine all of the ingredients in a large bowl.
3.   Pour mixture into a slow cooker and cook on high for 2-3 hours or until hot and bubbly.

Slow Cooker Bacon Ranch Potatoes

Servings: 8

What you need:
6 slices of bacon
3 lbs red potatoes, chopped
1 1/2 cups shredded cheddar cheese
1 tbsp ranch seasoning
2 tbsp chopped chives

What to do:
1.   Cook and crumble the bacon.
2.   Place the potatoes into the slow cooker and sprinkle them with cheese, ranch seasoning, and bacon.
3.   Cover and cook for 7-8 hours on low or 4 hours on high.
4.   Serve garnished with chives.

Strawberry Bacon Salad

Servings: 4

What you need:
1/2 head of romaine lettuce
4 cups spinach
1/2 cup toasted almonds
8-10 slices of cooked bacon, crumbled
2 cups sliced strawberries

What to do:
1. Chop the romaine lettuce into small pieces and place in a large bowl.
2. Mix the almonds and bacon crumbles into the bowl with the lettuce.
3. Add strawberries just before serving.
4. Serve with poppy seed dressing.

Egg in a Nest

Servings: 2

What you need:
2 slices of bread
2 tbsp butter
2 eggs
Salt and pepper, to taste

What to do:
1. Add the butter to a medium sized skillet over medium heat.
2. Cut a hole from the center of each slice of bread. You can use a drinking glass or a cookie cutter.
3. Place the bread slices in the pan and toast for a minute or two then flip.
4. Crack an egg into the center of each piece of toast.
5. Cook until the eggs are set.
6. Sprinkle with salt and pepper before serving.

Scrambled Eggs

Servings: 1-2

What you need:
1 tbsp butter
3 eggs
1/4 tsp salt
1/2 tsp butter
1/4 tsp black pepper

What to do:
1. Melt 1 tbsp of butter in a 10-inch non-stick skillet over medium-low heat.
2. Crack 3 eggs into a medium bowl and gently whisk with a fork until the whites and yolks are barely combined.
3. Pour the eggs into the skillet.
4. Let the eggs sit in the skillet until they begin to stick to the bottom of the skillet, about 30 seconds.
5. Begin stirring the eggs with a wooden spoon. Stir for 3-4 minutes.
6. Add 1/4 tsp of salt, 1/2 tsp of butter, 1/4 tsp of black pepper to the eggs and stir and cook for another 1-2 minutes.
7. Transfer to a plate and serve.

Brown Sugar Bacon

Servings: 4

What you need:
1 package bacon
1 cup brown sugar
1 tsp cayenne pepper

What to do:
1.   Preheat your oven to 375 degrees F.
2.   Line a large baking sheet with foil.
3.   In a shallow bowl, mix together the brown sugar and cayenne pepper.
4.   Dredge the bacon in the brown sugar mixture and lay each slice on the foil lined pan.
5.   Bake for 15-20 minutes or until bacon is crisp.
6.   Cool on a wire rack.

Sausage Breakfast Casserole

Servings: 4

What you need:
1 package of crescent rolls
1 lb ground sausage, browned and drained
6 eggs, beaten
2 cups shredded cheddar cheese

What to do:
1.   Preheat your oven to 350 degrees F.
2.   Spray a 9x13 inch pan with non-stick cooking spray.
3.   Roll the crescent rolls into the bottom of the pan.
4.   Top the rolls with the sausage in an even layer.
5.   Evenly pour the eggs over the sausage.
6.   Sprinkle the cheese evenly over the sausage and eggs.
7.   Bake for 30 minutes or until eggs are set.

Easy Powdered Sugar Donuts

Servings: 6

What you need:
2 7.5-oz rolls of canned biscuits
2 cups powdered sugar
Canola oil

What to do:
1. Pour an inch of canola oil into a heavy skillet and heat over medium heat on your stove.
2. Place a sheet of wax paper or parchment paper on your counter.
3. Unroll the biscuits and place them on the paper.
4. With a rolling pin or a jar, flatten out each biscuit.
5. Use a plastic bottle cap and make a donut hole in the center of each flattened roll.
6. When the oil is hot, place a few donuts in the skillet at a time. Don't overcrowd the skillet.
7. Let them cook for a minute or two and flip them with a fork.
8. Cook on each side until the donuts are golden brown, then transfer to a plate lined with paper towels to drain off some of the oil.
9. Place two cups of powdered sugar in a gallon zip lock bag.
10. After all of the donuts are cooked, place a few of them at a time in the zip lock bag, seal the bag and shake until they are covered completely.
11. Remove the donuts from the bag and repeat until all donuts are covered.
12. Serve warm.

Cinnamon Roll Waffles

Servings: 4

What you need:
1 can cinnamon roll dough

What to do:
1.   Heat your waffle maker.
2.   Separate the cinnamon rolls and set aside the icing.
3.   Spray your heated waffle maker and place one roll in and close the lid. Cook for about 2-3 minutes or until cinnamon roll is cooked through. Repeat until all cinnamon rolls are done.
4.   Remove the lid from the icing and microwave the icing for 15-20 seconds.
5.   Drizzle the icing over the cinnamon roll waffles before serving.

Southwestern Scrambled Eggs

Servings: 1-2

What you need:
3 eggs
1 tbsp milk
1/4 cup shredded cheese
1/4 cup black beans
1/4 cup salsa

What to do:
1. Spray a non-stick skillet with cooking spray and heat over medium-high heat.
2. Crack the eggs into a small bowl and whisk with a fork. Stir in the milk.
3. Pour the eggs into the heated pan.
4. When the eggs begin to cook, begin to stir them with a wooden spoon.
5. Add the black beans and continue to stir.
6. When eggs are done, transfer them to a plate.
7. Top with salsa and serve.

Blueberry Coconut Bars

Servings: 15

What you need:
2 cups sweetened coconut
2 cups blueberries
1/4 cup maple syrup
2 tsp ground vanilla beans

What to do:
1. Place all of the ingredients in your food processor and mix until smooth.
2. Line a square baking dish with parchment paper, extending it over the sides.
3. Pour the mixture into the baking dish and spread it evenly.
4. Gently press the mixture down using the extended sides of the parchment paper.
5. Refrigerate for 30 minutes, then slice and serve or store in the refrigerator in an airtight container.

Slow Cooker Pancake Bake

Servings: 4

What you need:
1 cup Bisquick
1/2 cup milk
1 egg
1/3 cup sugar
1 tbsp cinnamon

What to do:
1. Spray your slow cooker with nonstick spray or a place a liner in it.
2. In a medium bowl, whisk together the Bisquick, milk, and egg until there are no lumps.
3. Stir together the cinnamon and sugar in another bowl.
4. Pour the Bisquick mixture into the bottom of your slow cooker.
5. Sprinkle the cinnamon and sugar mixture over the top.
6. Cook for 1 hour to 1 1/2 hours or until the center is cooked through.

Slow Cooker Cinnamon Roll Casserole

Servings: 6

What you need:
2 12-oz tubes of cinnamon rolls, cut into 4 pieces each
4 eggs
1/2 cup whipping cream
3 tbsp maple syrup
2 tsp vanilla

What to do:
1. Spray your slow cooker with cooking spray or line it with a liner.
2. Place half of the cinnamon roll pieces into the bottom of your slow cooker. Make sure the bottom is completely covered.
3. In a small bowl, whisk together the eggs, cream, syrup, and vanilla.
4. Pour the mixture over the cinnamon rolls.
5. Place the remaining cinnamon roll pieces in the slow cooker and spoon 1 packet of the icing over the top.
6. Cook on low for 3 hours or until the sides are golden brown.
7. Drizzle the other packet of icing over the top before serving.

Slow Cooker French Toast

Servings: 4

What you need:
1/2 loaf of cinnamon bread
6 eggs
1 cup milk
1 tbsp brown sugar
1 tsp vanilla

What to do:
1. Spray your slow cooker with non-stick cooking spray.
2. In a large mixing bowl, whisk together the eggs, milk, brown sugar, and vanilla.
3. Dip each slice of bread into the egg mixture and then place it in your slow cooker.
4. Pour any remaining egg mixture on top of the bread in the slow cooker.
5. Cook on low 6-8 hours.
6. Serve with fresh fruit, whipped cream, or syrup.

Slow Cooker Blueberry Cobbler

Servings: 4

What you need:
1 18-oz yellow cake mix
3 cups frozen or fresh blueberries
1 stick butter
1/4 tsp cinnamon

What to do:
1.   Place the blueberries in your slow cooker.
2.   Sprinkle the cake mix onto the blueberries.
3.   Slice the butter and put it over the cake mix.
4.   Sprinkle with cinnamon.
5.   Cook on low for 4 hours.

Slow Cooker Cherry Dump Cake

Servings: 4

What you need:
21 oz can of cherry pie filling
1 15-oz yellow cake mix
1 stick butter
1/2 cup walnuts

What to do:
1.   Pour the cherry pie filling into your slow cooker.
2.   Sprinkle the cake mix over the cherries.
3.   Cut the butter into slices and put over the cake mix.
4.   Sprinkle on the walnuts.
5.   Cook on low for 4 hours.

Slow Cooker Bread Pudding

Servings: 4

What you need:
10 slices raisin cinnamon swirl bread, cut into cubes
1 14-oz can sweetened condensed milk
1 cup water
1 tsp vanilla
5 eggs, beaten

What to do:
1. Place the bread cubes into your slow cooker.
2. Mix the sweetened condensed milk, water, vanilla, and eggs together in a bowl and pour the mixture over the bread.
3. Stir to coat the bread evenly.
4. Cook on low for 3-4 hours or until set.

Slow Cooker Peach Cobbler

Servings: 4

What you need:
1 18-oz yellow cake mix
3 cups frozen or fresh peaches, sliced
1 stick butter
1/4 tsp cinnamon

What to do:
1. Place the peaches in your slow cooker.
2. Sprinkle the cake mix onto the peaches.
3. Slice the butter and put it over the cake mix.
4. Sprinkle with cinnamon.
5. Cook on low for 4 hours.

Slow Cooker Apple Dump Cake

Servings: 4

What you need:
21 oz can of apple pie filling
1 15-oz yellow cake mix
1 stick butter
1/2 cup walnuts

What to do:
1.   Pour the apple pie filling into your slow cooker.
2.   Sprinkle the cake mix over the apples.
3.   Cut the butter into slices and put over the cake mix.
4.   Sprinkle on the walnuts.
5.   Cook on low for 4 hours.

About the Author

Hannie's vision is to write a series of recipe books, each focusing on one theme or one type of food that could can be EASILY prepared by someone who wouldn't be considered your typical cook. She urges her readers to feel welcome to share recipes, thoughts, and ideas with her and any feedback is encouraged.

For more recipe books visit www.hanniepscott.com

Made in the USA
San Bernardino, CA
18 November 2016